Collins
INTERNATIONAL
PRIMARY

Wellbeing
Student's Book 6

William Collins' dream of knowledge for all began with the publication of his first book in 1819.

A self-educated mill worker, he not only enriched millions of lives, but also founded a flourishing publishing house. Today, staying true to this spirit, Collins books are packed with inspiration, innovation and practical expertise.

They place you at the centre of a world of possibility and give you exactly what you need to explore it.

Collins. Freedom to teach.

Published by Collins

An imprint of HarperCollins*Publishers*
The News Building, 1 London Bridge Street, London,
SE1 9GF, UK

HarperCollins*Publishers*
Macken House, 39/40 Mayor Street Upper, Dublin 1 D01 C9W8

Browse the complete Collins catalogue at
collins.co.uk

© HarperCollins*Publishers* Limited 2024

10 9 8 7 6 5 4 3 2 1

ISBN 978-0-00-864524-3

British Library Cataloguing-in-Publication Data
A catalogue record for this publication is available from the British Library.

Cambridge International copyright material in this publication is reproduced under licence and remains the intellectual property of Cambridge Assessment International Education.

Third-party websites and resources referred to in this publication have not been endorsed by Cambridge International Education.

Endorsement indicates that a resource has passed Cambridge International Education's rigorous quality-assurance process and is suitable to support the delivery of a Cambridge curriculum framework. However, endorsed resources are not the only suitable materials available to support teaching and learning, and are not essential to achieve the qualification. Resource lists found on the Cambridge website will include this resource and other endorsed resources.

Any example answers to questions taken from past question papers, practice questions, accompanying marks and mark schemes included in this resource have been written by the authors and are for guidance only. They do not replicate examination papers. In examinations the way marks are awarded may be different. Any references to assessment and/or assessment preparation are the publisher's interpretation of the curriculum framework requirements. Examiners will not use endorsed resources as a source of material for any assessment set by Cambridge International Education.

While the publishers have made every attempt to ensure that advice on the qualification and its assessment is accurate, the official curriculum framework, specimen assessment materials and any associated assessment guidance materials produced by the awarding body are the only authoritative source of information and should always be referred to for definitive guidance.

Our approach is to provide teachers with access to a wide range of high-quality resources that suit different styles and types of teaching and learning.

For more information about the endorsement process, please visit www.cambridgeinternational.org/endorsed-resources

Series editors: Kate Daniels and Victoria Pugh
Authors: Kate Daniels and Victoria Pugh
Publisher: Elaine Higgleton
Product Manager: Cathy Martin
Product developer: Roisin Leahy
Development and copy editor: Jo Kemp
Proofreader: Claire Throp
Permissions researcher: Rachel Thorne
Illustrations: Jouve India Ltd.
Cover designer: Amparo Barrera, Kneath Associates and Gordon MacGilp
Typesetter: Sam Vail, Ken Vail Graphic Design
Production controller: Sarah Hovell
Printed and bound by Martins the Printers

MIX
Paper | Supporting responsible forestry
FSC™ C007454
www.fsc.org

This book is produced from independently certified FSC™ paper to ensure responsible forest management.

For more information visit: www.harpercollins.co.uk/green

Access and download editable versions of these resources and the accompanying PowerPoint presentations at collins.co.uk/internationalresources

We are grateful to the following teachers for providing feedback on the resources as they were developed:
Ms Hema Gehani and Ms Seema Desai at Colours Innovation Academy, Ms Manjari Tennakoon and Ms Surani Maithripala at Gateway Colleges, and Preeti Roychoudhury, Farishta Dastur Mukerji, Spriha Patronobis and Sukonna Halder at Calcutta International School.

Contents

Hello and welcome to Wellbeing Stage 6's student's book!

Dealing with feelings

Despite the exciting times ahead you probably have all sorts of feelings going on and these might feel quite mixed up. You might be a bit excited about the changes ahead, but you might feel nervous too. Perhaps you feel ready to move on, but worried about making new friends?

Never fear, this workbook is here to help you.

It will help you to name and understand your feelings and it will help you learn ways to feel calmer and more in control.

Exercising your mind

You do Physical Education every week at school to make your body strong and healthy. Physical exercise can help you do lots of things well (like dance and lift and heal).

When you do emotional exercises like the ones in this workbook, the same thing happens: you will also get stronger but in your mind, rather than in your body.

When you exercise your mind, you get better at things like managing your feelings. You also begin to find solving problems easier and learn to bounce back when things go wrong.

Mind exercises are amazing, and they are scientifically PROVEN to work.

Power tools!

This wellbeing workbook is powerful!

It will teach you all sorts of things that will help you in life, such as how to:

- calm yourself down
- cheer yourself up
- Ask for help
- Stand up for yourself
- get on well with others
- worry less
- feel happier more often
- handle feeling stressed.

Once you know how, you will see that you can change how you think, how you feel and how you act all by yourself.

It feels brilliant to be able to help yourself. And once you have learned how, you will be able to handle whatever comes your way with a lot more confidence.

Emotional health tools are power tools that you can use your whole life – whenever you need them.

Doesn't that sound brilliant?

If you are ready, then let's make a start!

May your year ahead be as special as you are!

– Becky Goddard-Hill

Unit 6.1 Our emotions

What do you know?

- What might be happening in the picture?
- How might the child be feeling?
- How might she react to this?

In this unit, you will:

- Explore people's reactions to emotions.
- Consider a range of scenarios and how each character might feel and react.
- Create a booklet which gives information about the causes of stress and includes strategies to overcome it.

Lesson 1 Exploring emotions

Activity 1.1 How might they feel and react?

Look at each of the scenarios below. How might each of the characters be feeling? How might they react in these situations?

1.

Charlize and her dad planned to go swimming at the weekend. Charlize has been looking forward to it all week, but on Saturday morning, her dad gets called into work and he has to cancel the swimming. What emotions might Charlize be feeling? What emotions might her dad be feeling?

How might Charlize feel?

_____

_____

How might her dad feel?

_____

_____

2.

Paulo and his brother have just been told that they are going to a theme park. Paulo doesn't like rollercoasters, but he does love the characters and the food stalls. What emotions do you think he and his brother might be feeling?

How might Paulo feel?

_____

_____

How might his brother feel?

_____

_____

3.

Jeno has fallen out with his best friend. He has just texted him but his friend isn't replying. What emotions do you think Jeno is feeling?

How might Jeno feel?

_____

_____

How might his friend feel?

_____

_____

3

Lesson 2 How stress can affect our bodies

Activity 1.2a What is stress?

Draw a picture that represents stress. You can use colour, shape, scenarios or words to explore what stress is.

Lesson 2 How stress can affect our bodies

Activity 1.2b What might make people feel stressed?

Have you ever felt stressed? What made you feel this way?

What other things might cause people to feel stressed?

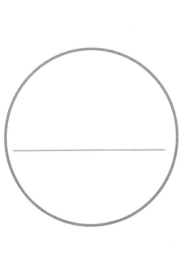

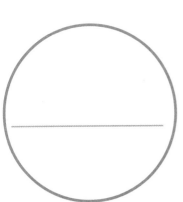

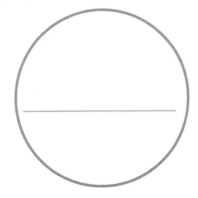

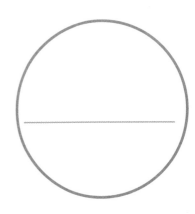

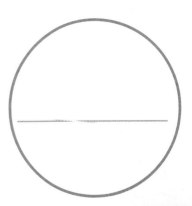

Lesson 3 Feeling worried

Activity 1.3a Times of change

What worries might students of your age have?

_____

_____

_____

What advice would you give?

_____

_____

_____

Choose one worry and create an advice page for students on how they could overcome this worry.

Lesson 3 Feeling worried

Activity 1.3b Reflection

Consider the emotions below and think about times when you have experienced each emotion or feeling. Complete the sentences below.

I feel happy when

_____

_____

_____

_____

I feel excited when

_____

_____

_____

_____

I feel overwhelmed when

_____

_____

_____

_____

I feel scared when

_____

_____

_____

_____

I feel hopeful when

_____

_____

_____

_____

I feel angry when

_____

_____

_____

_____

Unit reflection

Think about your lessons from this unit. Consider three key things you have learned and write them below.

1. _____

_____

2. _____

_____

3. _____

_____

What strategies might you use to calm down when you feel stressed? Make a mind map below.

Unit 6.2 Healthy minds

What do you know?

- What can you see in the photo?
- How might the man be feeling?

In this unit, you will:

- Discuss why it is important to relax.
- Take part in a debate about editing photos.
- Create a class exercise book.

Lesson 1 Self-care

Activity 2.1a What is your day like?

Fill in your daily schedule on this 24-hour diary. Be honest – no one is judging you.

Time (24-hr)	Activity	How does this activity make you feel?
00:00		
01:00		
02:00		
03:00		
04:00		
05:00		
06:00		
07:00		
08:00		
09:00		
10:00		
11:00		
12:00		
13:00		
14:00		
15:00		
16:00		
17:00		
18:00		
19:00		
20:00		
21:00		
22:00		
23:00		

Lesson 1 Self-care

Activity 2.1b How do you like to relax?

Try out some of the relaxation examples from the lesson.
Which ones did you like?

_____

_____

_____

_____

_____

What other ways of relaxing do you enjoy?

_____

_____

_____

_____

_____

_____

_____

Why is it important for us to relax?

_____

_____

_____

_____

Lesson 2 Comparing yourself with others

Activity 2.2a Photoshopping

Should it be made illegal to photoshop images which are posted online or used in advertising?

What are your thoughts? Write your ideas below.

Lesson 2 Comparing yourself with others

Activity 2.2b The big debate!

Use the space below to plan your debate. Make a note of your research points and which websites or books you used to find your information.

Lesson 3 What is so good about exercise and movement?

Activity 2.3a Instructions for great exercise

You are going to create a page for a class book called 'Our Favourite Ways to Exercise'.

1. Think of something that you love doing that will help your friends get fit.

2. Write or draw clear instructions to help them.

(You will need to include details such as whether they will need an adult with them, where it is going to take place, what they might need and how long it will take.)

My exercise:

_____

_____

_____

_____

_____

_____

_____

_____

Lesson 3 What is so good about exercise and movement?

Activity 2.3b Reflections

Consider what you have learned about exercise and movement in your lesson.

What are three key things you have learned today?

1.

2.

3.

Unit reflection

Take some time to really think about what you have learned over this unit.

What have you learned about the importance of taking time to relax, and strategies you can use to relax and feel mentally healthy?

Draw or write some interesting facts or reflections below. Are there any strategies which you might try to include in your day-to-day life to support your own healthy mind?

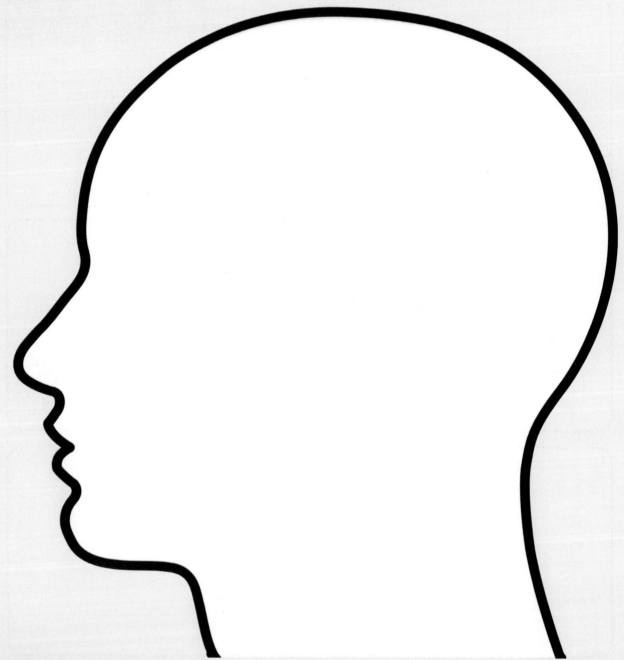

Unit 6.3 Medicines and health

What do you know?

● What is happening in the picture?

● How do you think each of the characters feel?

In this unit, you will:

● Create a poster of how you can support a friend who might be feeling down or be struggling with their mental health.

● Describe what medicines do and how they can be used safely.

● Create an information leaflet about how vaccinations work and why they are administered.

Lesson 1 What to do if I'm worried

Activity 3.1 Supporting a friend in need

Write down all the strategies which you might use to support a friend who is struggling with their mental health or feeling down.

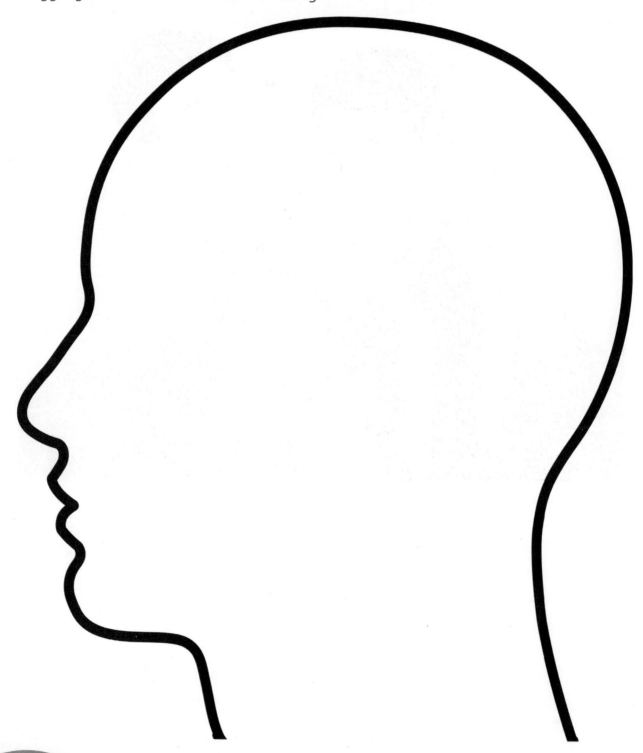

Lesson 2 Medicines and health

Activity 3.2a What should they do?

Read each of the scenarios and advise the characters what they should do.

> Max is at his grandma's house. He has a headache and wants to take some medicine to help it. He sees the medicine he is looking for. He doesn't want to bother his grandma as she is busy, so he thinks he should just take it himself. What should Max do?

_____

_____

_____

_____

_____

> Priah finds some tablets on the kitchen floor. What should she do?

_____

_____

_____

> Ajeet has a sore throat, so his friend offers him some of his throat syrup. What should Ajeet do?

_____

_____

_____

_____

Lesson 2 Medicines and health

Activity 3.2b Medicines quiz

Research the answers to the questions on your own or with a group.

1. Who discovered antibiotics?

_____

_____

2. What does an antiseptic do?

_____

_____

_____

_____

3. List three safety rules when storing or taking medicines.

_____

_____

_____

_____

4. What should you do if someone other than a trusted adult offers you drugs or medicine?

_____

_____

_____

_____

5. Tablets are the only form of medicine. True or false? Explain your answer.

_____

_____

_____

_____

Lesson 2 Medicines and health

Activity 3.2c Antibiotics

Read the extract below from the book *Surgery Through Time* to learn more about antibiotics today and answer the questions below in groups.

We now have many different antibiotics, used to kill different bacteria. But some bacteria are changing and are no longer killed by existing antibiotics. Scientists constantly look for new antibiotics.

Keeping hospitals very clean is even more important as antibiotics work better in clean conditions. Medical staff scrub themselves with soap and wear sterile clothes. Instruments are sterilised by boiling or radiation, and surfaces are all cleaned thoroughly with antiseptics.

– Anne Rooney

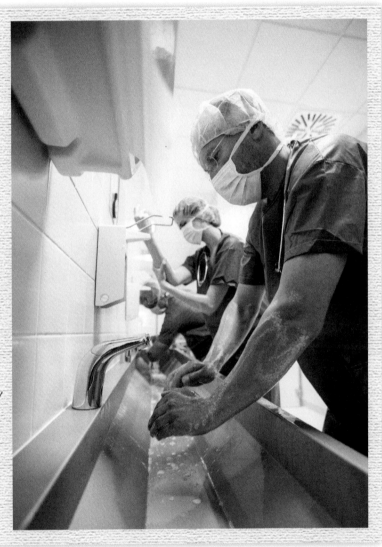

Consider and discuss these questions in your group.

1. How do you think antibiotics differ now from when they were discovered?

2. Why is it important that hospitals are clean and what do you think staff have to do to ensure that it is clean?

3. Why are scientists always looking for new antibiotics?

Lesson 3 Vaccinations

Activity 3.3a Edward Jenner fact file

Find out facts about Edward Jenner, his personal and professional life. Consider where and when he lived, what he studied and how he discovered vaccines.

Lesson 3 Vaccinations

Activity 3.3b Vaccination facts

List as many facts about vaccinations as you can below. Share these with your group. Did any group members have facts that you didn't?

Unit reflection

Consider what you have learned in this unit.
Write your reflections below.

1. What are medicines?

_____

_____

_____

_____

_____

_____

2. What can they do?

_____

_____

_____

_____

_____

_____

3. How can we keep medicines safe?

_____

_____

_____

_____

_____

4. Who could you go to if you were worried about the health of a friend?

_____

_____

_____

_____

_____

Unit 6.4 People and me

What do you know?
- What's happening with the toddlers in this picture?
- If you were their big sister or brother, how would you get them to resolve their conflict?

In this unit, you will:
- Consider stereotypes and how we can challenge them.
- Learn about conflict resolution.
- Find out about the six different types of peer pressure.

Lesson 1 Stereotypes

Activity 4.1a What do I know?

Everything I think
I know about stereotypes

Lesson 1 Stereotypes

Activity 4.1b Reflection

What did you learn or begin to think about from this activity?

Write down everything you remember and rank them in order of importance to you with number 1 being the least important.

1. _____
   _____
   _____
   _____

2. _____
   _____
   _____
   _____

3. _____
   _____
   _____
   _____

4. _____
   _____
   _____

5. _____
   _____
   _____

Lesson 2 When we fall out

Activity 4.2a When we fall out

Read this story about a family.

'I hate you!' shouted Najeeb as he slammed his bedroom door and flung himself on his bed. His little sister was SOOOOO stupid! He could hear her crying loudly downstairs.

The door opened and his mum came in. 'Habib Albi, what has got into you? Your sister is so sad! This is not like you!'

Mum sat down on his bed and waited for him to talk.

Najeeb started to cry – he felt angry and sad all at once. He knew it wasn't like him. He loved his little sister, Kyra; she was funny and sweet, and they were normally good friends.

He told his mum how she was running around in the living room being silly and she had fallen over him and broken his model – the one he had nearly finished after working on it for months. She had hurt herself, but Najeeb hadn't cared... He had felt so cross with her that he had shouted really loudly in her face and pushed her roughly out the way and then she had screamed back at him.

Mum understood why Najeeb was so upset but she wasn't happy with how he had reacted. She told him to calm down and then they would talk about it all together...

Talk to your partner and write down your answers.

Why did Najeeb and Kyra fall out?

_____

_____

How did they act towards one another when they were hurt and angry?

_____

_____

What can they do to sort it out?

_____

_____

Lesson 2 When we fall out

Activity 4.2b When we fall out

Write answers to these questions.

1. What have I learned in this lesson?

_____

_____

_____

_____

_____

_____

2. Can I list all the positive things people can do when they fall out?

_____

_____

_____

_____

_____

_____

3. What can I change or try next time I fall out with someone?

_____

_____

_____

_____

_____

_____

_____

_____

Lesson 3 Under pressure

Activity 4.3a Your pressure relief doodle page

Lesson 3 Under pressure

Activity 4.3b Reflection

You learned about peer pressure today.

1. What is peer pressure?

_____

_____

_____

2. What were the six different types of peer pressure?

_____

_____

_____

3. In what sort of situations might we experience peer pressure? Write some examples.

_____

_____

_____

4. What strategies could you use if you felt you were being pressured to do something you didn't want to do?

_____

_____

_____

5. Is there anything that has worried you or you would like to learn more about regarding peer pressure?

_____

_____

_____

Unit reflection

Reflect back to the unit introduction and revisit the question, "If you were the toddlers' big sister or brother, how would you get them to resolve their conflict?"

Read back over how you answered that question and ask yourself if you would change anything you wrote and, if so, what?

Use the space below to write what you would do and say now.

Unit 6.5 Community and choices

What do you know?

● What can you see in the picture?

● What do you think is happening?

● Who is involved in the picture?

In this unit, you will:

● Consider what your own boundaries are and how you can respect the boundaries of others.

● Create a map of the local community showing all of the community groups you belong to.

● Design a community centre which will benefit all local people.

Lesson 1 I have choices

Activity 5.1a Decisions, decisions

Consider choices that have been made in your life. How were these decisions made? Who made them?

What is the decision?	Who makes the decision?	Why do they make the decision?

Lesson1 I have choices

Activity 5.1b Personal boundaries

Write or draw an ending for each scenario.

> Alice and Maria are sitting on the carpet in the classroom, listening to the teacher. Alice keeps playing with Maria's hair and she doesn't like it, but she doesn't want to be rude. What could she do?

Devon is at a family party and is about to leave with his family. His mum wants him to hug his Aunty Sandra goodbye, but he doesn't want to. What should he do?

Jamil and Max are playing together in the playground. Jamil wants to stand very close to Max, but Max keeps moving away. What should Max do?

Lesson 2 I belong to my community

Activity 5.2 Community map

Work with your group to consider all of the communities you belong to. These might be sport teams, music groups, places of worship, and so on. Draw or write about each one below.

Communities I belong to

Lesson 3 It's everyone's community

Activity 5.3 Design task

Design a community centre or space which would benefit everyone. Identify all of the key features of your community centre on the next page.

Write all of the key design features of your community centre or space below.

Unit reflection

Spend some time reflecting on what community means to you. Can you think of some words connected with community? These might be words which link to how being part of a community makes you feel, what communities can do or different types of communities. Write words starting with the first letter of the word community below.

C _____

O _____

M _____

M _____

U _____

N _____

I _____

T _____

Y _____

Now spend some time reflecting on what decisions are yours to make, and why, when you are younger, other people make some decisions for you.

_____

_____

_____

_____

_____

_____

_____

_____

_____

_____

Unit 6.6 Our safety

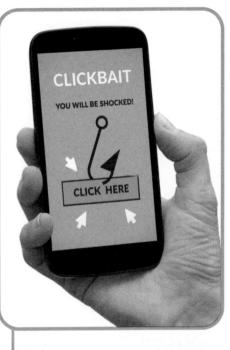

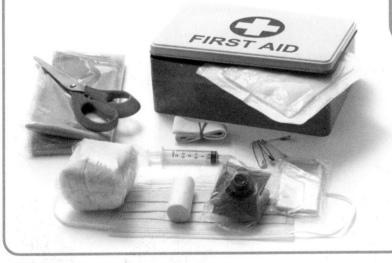

What do you know?

● What do we need passwords and PINs for?

● What do you think clickbait is? Draw what you think it is. (If you don't know, have a guess!)

In this unit, you will:

● Learn about passwords and PINs.

● Learn about clickbait.

● Learn about first aid.

Lesson 1 PINs and passwords

Activity 6.1 Designing passwords

See how many different unique passwords you can design below. One has been done for you: sUntrE!e4Brick. This has been made using three random words: sun, tree and brick. There are lower-case and upper-case letters and two characters (! and 4) mixed in to make it more complex.

Now it's your turn! How many can you make?

- _____
- _____
- _____
- _____
- _____
- _____
- _____
- _____

Lesson 2 First aid

Activity 6.2a What can I do to help?

Choose one of the common first aid situations you have discussed as a class and research how you can help a patient in this situation.

I am researching how to help someone who

I need to

What else do I need to think about?

Lesson 2 First aid

Lesson 6.2b The recovery position

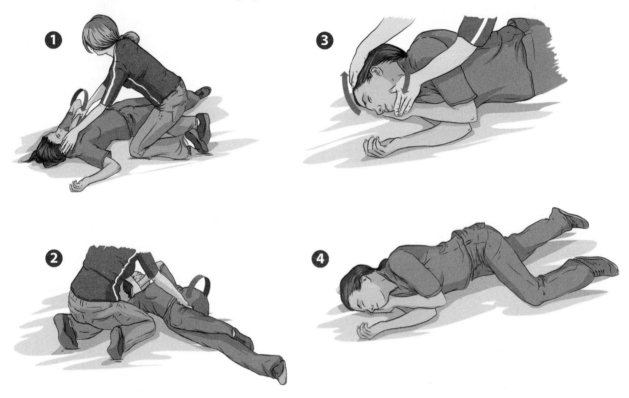

- With the patient lying on their back, place the nearest arm to you at a right angle to their body.

- Move the other arm across the chest with the back of the hand underneath the patient's cheek.

- Bend the leg furthest away, bringing it towards you until the foot is flat on the floor.

- Holding the bent leg and with your hand underneath the patient's cheek, roll the patient onto their side.

- Tilt their head back to open their airways.

Lesson 2 First aid

Lesson 6.2c The role of a paramedic

Read the extract below from *Dani Binns Practical Paramedic* to learn more about the role of a paramedic.

"What happened?" Dani asked the boy.

"She was riding into the park, quite fast. She swerved to avoid me and flew over the handlebars. I think she landed on her head. I told her not to move. Then I called for an ambulance," he replied.

"You did the right thing, telling her not to move," said Tai. "If she landed on her head, she might have injured her neck or back. That's very serious."

Asha checked the girl's pulse and breathing. Then she put an inflating cuff around the girl's arm to check her blood pressure. Tai shone a mini torch in her eyes to check her reactions.

Have you learned anything useful from reading this extract? If so, what is it?

Lesson 3 Clickbait

Activity 6.3a Clickbait

Would you be tempted to click on any of these? Why? What words do they use to draw you in? Discuss this with a partner, then circle the words and add notes to show all the strategies they use to tempt people to click to take you to their web page.

Lesson 3 Clickbait

Activity 6.3b The dangers of clickbait

Unit reflection

What three things do you know now you have completed this unit?

Unit 6.7 Tackling the tough stuff

What do you know?

- What does this picture represent to you?
- How might life sometimes feel tough, like there is a storm cloud blocking out the sun?
- How can noticing the 'silver lining' help when you are in challenging times?

In this unit, you will:

- Consider how we deal with loss and change.
- Think about how we deal with mistakes.
- Think about how we can breeze exams!

Lesson 1 Moving

Activity 7.1a Top tips for moving

How could you make someone who is new to the country feel more welcome or settled?

Write down your top five strategies to support them.

1. _____

_____

_____

2. _____

_____

_____

3. _____

_____

_____

4. _____

_____

_____

5. _____

_____

_____

Lesson 1 Moving

Activity 7.1b Interview questions

You will be interviewing staff within your school who have moved areas or countries. What questions would you like to ask them so that you have a better understanding of how people feel when they move? What helped them to feel more settled?

INTERVIEW

1. _____

_____

_____

_____

2. _____

_____

_____

_____

3. _____

_____

_____

_____

4. _____

_____

_____

_____

5. _____

_____

_____

_____

Lesson 2 Never give up

Activity 7.2a Practising and giving your best

Practice, determination and giving your best – this is what Michael Jordan's parents said were the things that would help to make him a winner. How can you apply this to your goals?

Draw a picture below of you achieving your goal. Around the outside of your picture answer the questions that are displayed on the slide.

Lesson 2 Never give up

Activity 7.2b Reflection

● Has this lesson helped you to see mistakes in a different way? If so, how?

_____

_____

_____

● Write or draw below all that you have learned, or what you now think about mistakes.

Lesson 3 Exams, I'm ready!

Activity 7.3a Metacognition

What do you remember about metacognition? Write or draw below what you have learned and how your metacognition journey is going. Have you noticed anything about your thinking or used any of the skills you have learned, such as visualisation?

Lesson 3 Exams, I'm ready!

Activity 7.3b Reflection

How can you use the skills you have learned about in this lesson in exams?

Unit reflection: Relax

You've learned about how to tackle tricky things in this unit.

Here's a page to colour in and calm you if you are feeling anxious or worried, or just for fun, now or in the future. Enjoy!

Unit 6.8 The world we live in

What do you know?

● Look closely. What can you see in this picture?

● What do you love about our world? Draw all the things you love.

In this unit, you will:

● Learn about the 4 Rs of waste reduction.

● Understand what ethical consumerism is.

● Consider the beauty of our diverse world.

Lesson 1 What's the good news?

Activity 8.1a What I know

Create a mind map and write down everything you can think of to do with sustainability, sustainable development goals and the 4 Rs – Reduce, Recycle, Reuse, Repurpose. If you have any questions, you can write these in the space below.

Sustainability

Questions I have about sustainability issues:

_____

_____

_____

_____

Lesson 1 What's the good news?

Activity 8.1b A good news story

Daily **NEWS**

Lesson 2 Fairtrade

Activity 8.2a Fairtrade chocolate advert script

Lesson 2 Fairtrade

Activity 8.2b Fairtrade illustration

Draw an illustration below for a Fairtrade advert for newspapers and magazines or for public transport.

Lesson 3 Diverse communities

Activity 8.3a My interview

Write the questions you are going to ask in your interview. Try to find out as much as you can about the person's culture. For example, you could ask questions about language or dialect, history, race, food, music, religious beliefs, festivals and celebrations or anything else you wish to ask them. (Use the back of the sheet if you need more room.)

1. _____

_____

_____

_____

2. _____

_____

_____

_____

3. _____

_____

_____

_____

4. _____

_____

_____

_____

5. _____

_____

_____

_____

6. _____

_____

_____

_____

Lesson 3 Diverse communities

Activity 8.3b Making a kinder world

If you were in charge of the world, what would you do to make it a kinder place for everyone to live in?

Unit reflection

What changes are you going to make in your life based on what you have learned in this unit?

Go back through your workbook to help you remember.

_____

_____

_____

_____

_____

_____

_____

_____

_____

_____

Slide 2 boxstock / Shutterstock, **4.8.1** SB p. 57 max dallocco/ Shutterstock, PPT slide 1 Preres/ Shutterstock, slide 2 Prapat Aowsakorn/ Shutterstock, slide 3 Studio_G/ Shutterstock, SB p. 58, PPT, WS Studio_G/ Shutterstock, **4.8.2** PPT slide 1 & SB p59 © HarperCollins Publisher 2020, slides 2 & 3 (tl) AlenKadr/ Shutterstock, slides 2 & 3 (tr) Teerasak Ladnongkhun/ Shutterstock, slides 2 & 3 (bl) Mike Truchon/ Shutterstock 4.8.2 (br) M88/ Shutterstock, slide 5 Part of Design/ Shutterstock, SB p. 60 (t) frank60/ Shutterstock, (b) Rich Carey/ Shutterstock, SB p. 61 Maryshot/ Shutterstock, **4.8.3** PPT Slide 1 Lightspring/ Shutterstock, **5.1.1** SB p. 1 (tl) Atomic Roderick/ Shutterstock, (tr) Jasmine Creation/ Shutterstock, (b) mentalmind/ Shutterstock, PPT Slide 1 asiandelight/ Shutterstock, Slide 2 Michael Kraus/ Shutterstock, **5.1.2** PPT Slide 1 (l) Sabrina Bracher/ Shutterstock, (r) Queenmoonlite Studio/ Shutterstock, Slide 2 Natalie Board/ Shutterstock, Slide 3 Andrekart Photography/ Shutterstock, Slide 4 Chay_Tee/ Shutterstock, Slide 5 © HarperCollins Publishers 2020, **5.1.3** SB p.6 HowLettery/ Shutterstock, p.7 CallMeTak/ Shutterstock WS HowLettery/Shutterstock, PPT Slide 1 Rambleron/Vecteezy, Slide 2 (t) Ground Picture/ Shutterstock, (bl) Godong/ Alamy Stock Photo, (br) James Kirkikis/ Shutterstock, Slide 3 Microstocker.Pro/ Shutterstock, Slide 4 GoodStudio/ Shutterstock, Slide 4 TALVA/ Shutterstock, **5.2.1** SB p.9 KlingSup/ Shutterstock, PPT Slide 1 Kolonko/ Shutterstock, Slide 2 metamorworks/ Shutterstock, Slide 3 Ground Picture/ Shutterstock, Slide 4 (tl) minizen/ Shutterstock, (t) Net Vector/ Shutterstock, (tr) giedre vaitekune/ Shutterstock, (bl) Yuri Chuprakov/ Shutterstock, (b) Simakova Mariia/ Shutterstock, (br) backUp/ Shutterstock, **5.2.2** PPT Slide 1 Kaspars Grinvalds/Shutterstock, Slide 2 Vladimir Gjorgiev/ Shutterstock, Slide 3 Africa Studio/ Shutterstock, Slide 4 Mariia Boiko/ Shutterstock, Slide 5 Nor Gal/ Shutterstock, SB p.13 karakotsya/ Shutterstock, **5.2.3** PPT Slide 1 (l) & SB p.16 Viktorija Reuta/ Shutterstock, Slide 1 (r) maglyvi/ Shutterstock, Slide 2 & 3 Daisy Daisy/ Shutterstock, Slide 2 + 3 Timolina/ Shutterstock, Slide 2 + 3 Hung Chung Chih/ Shutterstock, Slide 2 + 3 alif_Osman/ Shutterstock, Slide 2 + 3 ESB Professional/ Shutterstock, Slide 3 Wahyu Ananda/ Shutterstock, Slide 3 wavebreakmedia/ Shutterstock, Slide 4 (l) stockpexel/ Shutterstock, (r) wavebreakmedia/ Shutterstock, Slide 4 PeopleImages.com – Yuri A/ Shutterstock, SB p.15 (l) Aleksandr Merg/ Shutterstock, WS 5.2.3a Aleksandr Merg/ Shutterstock, SB p. 15 (r) woocat/ Shutterstock, WS 5.2.3a woocat/ Shutterstock, WS 5.2.3b, SB p.16 Viktorija Reuta/Shutterstock, **5.3.1** SB p.17 (tl) pixelheadphoto digitalskillet/ Shutterstock, (tr) F01 PHOTO/ Shutterstock, (b) fizkes/ Shutterstock, PPT Slide 1 (l) fizkes/ Shutterstock, (r) Nowaczyk/ Shutterstock, Slide 2 (l) SeventyFour/ Shutterstock, (r) Solid photos/ Shutterstock, Slide 3 (tl) fizkes/ Shutterstock, (r) Krakenimages.com/ Shutterstock, (bl) MalikNalik/ Shutterstock, SB p.18 (t) & PPT Slide 4 PixyPen/ Shutterstock, TG WS PixyPen/ Shutterstock, SB p.18 (b) Colorfuel Studio/ Shutterstock, TG WS Colorfuel Studio/ Shutterstock, **5.3.2** PPT Slide 1 ANURAK PONGPATIMET/ Shutterstock, Slide 2 + 3 (bl) Lakmal Ditmax/ Shutterstock, PPT Slide 2 (tr) Lapina/ Shutterstock, Slide 2 (br) New Africa/ Shutterstock, Slide 3 (t) Carkhe/ Shutterstock, (l) Kolonko/ Shutterstock, TG WS 5.3.2, **5.3.3** PPT Slide 1 (b) WEB-DESIGN/ Shutterstock, Slide 3 Studio Barcelona/ Shutterstock, Slide 5 Frenggo/ Shutterstock, PPT Slide 6 katsuba_art/Shutterstock, **5.4.1** SB p.25 Rawpixel.com/ Shutterstock, p.26 Vegorus/ Shutterstock, WS Vegorus/ Shutterstock,SB p.27 Monkey Business Images/ Shutterstock, PPT Slide 1 (tl) IndianFaces/ Shutterstock, (tr) SALMONNEGRO-STOCK/ Shutterstock, (bl) Aleem Zahid Khan/ Shutterstock, (br) Yuri Dondish/ Shutterstock, Slide 3 wellphoto/ Shutterstock, **5.4.2** PPT Slide 1 & SB p.29 afry_harvy/ Shutterstock, Slide 2 Pressmaster/ Shutterstock, Slide 3 LightField Studios/ Shutterstock, SB p.30 Reprinted by permission of HarperCollins Publishers Ltd © 2022 A. M. Dassu, **5.4.3** PPT Slides 4–6 Intellson/ Shutterstock, **5.5.1** SB p.33 SewCreamStudio/ Shutterstock, PPT Slide 2 (tl) Prostock-studio/ Shutterstock, (tr) HAKINMHAN/ Shutterstock, (bl) Image bug/ Shutterstock, (br) pixelheadphoto digitalskillet/ Shutterstock, Slide 3 vectornation/ Shutterstock, Slide 4 Pixel-Shot/ Shutterstock, **5.5.2** PPT Slide 1 (tl) memej/ Shutterstock, (t) Yukhym Turkin/ Shutterstock, (tr) Aletkina Olga/ Shutterstock, (bl) Glinskaja Olga/ Shutterstock, (br) woocat/Shutterstock, Slide 2 Sudowoodo/ Shutterstock, Slide 4 MARI_NAD/ Shutterstock, **5.5.3** PPT Slide 1 & SB p.37 Elena Zajchikova/ Shutterstock, Slide 2 tangguhpro/ Shutterstock, Slide 3 Seqoya/ Shutterstock, Slide 4 & SB p.38 Victoria 1/ Shutterstock, SB p.38 Maksym Drozd/ Shutterstock, **5.6.1** SB p.41 WESTOCK PRODUCTIONS/ Shutterstock, PPT Slide 3 & SB p.42 Pungu x/ Shutterstock, WS Pungu x/ Shutterstock, PPT Slide 5 Pixel-Shot/ Shutterstock, Slide 6 Roman Arbuzov/ Shutterstock, **5.6.2** SB p.45 (t) TR STOK/ Shutterstock, (b) Gatien GREGORI/ Shutterstock, SB p.45 Text Reprinted by permission of HarperCollins Publishers Ltd © 2022 Mio Debnam, PPT Slide 1 trgrowth/ Shutterstock, Slide 2 Phonix_a Pk.sarote/ Shutterstock, Slide 3 Pakhnyushchy/ Shutterstock, Slide 4 kornnphoto/ Shutterstock, Slide 5 Dmitry Naumov/ Shutterstock, Slide 6 AntiD/ Shutterstock, **5.6.3** SB p.47 Reprinted by permission of HarperCollins Publishers Ltd © 2023 Jo Cotterill, SB p.48 (t) Monster Ztudio/ Shutterstock, (l) Rafael Croonen/ Shutterstock, (b) Luce Altra/ Shutterstock, PPT Slide 1 SynthEx/ Shutterstock, Slide 2 HamaVision/Shutterstock, Slide 3 (tr) smx12/Shutterstock, (r) Oleksandra Klestova/ Shutterstock, (br) Toxa2x2/ Shutterstock, Slide 4 Aleksandra Suzi/ Shutterstock, **5.7.1** SB pp. 49&56 Darkdiamond67/ Shutterstock, PPT Slide 1 Food Impressions/ Shutterstock, Slide 3 winyuu/ Shutterstock, Slide 4 Petar Dojranliev/ Shutterstock, **5.7.2** SB p.53 GoodStudio/ Shutterstock, PPT Slide 1 Olena Yakobchuk/ Shutterstock, Slide 3 (tl) Winai Tepsuttinun/ Shutterstock, (t) Elnur/ Shutterstock, (l) luchschenF/ Shutterstock, (t) rvlsoft/ Shutterstock, (c) Passakorn sakulphan/ Shutterstock, (r) Ilina Yuliia/ Shutterstock, (tr) Sergio33/ Shutterstock, (bl) Volodymyr Krasyuk/ Shutterstock, (b) Pixel-Shot/ Shutterstock, (br) Chonlatee42/ Shutterstock, Slide 4 horst friedrichs / Alamy Stock Photo, **5.7.3** PPT Slide 1 ImageFlow/ Shutterstock, Slide 4 Serhii Bobyk/ Shutterstock, Slide 5 Red Fox studio/ Shutterstock, **5.8.1** SB p.57 nexus 7/ Shutterstock, p.58 piotr_pabijan/ Shutterstock, p59 &

Acknowledgements

We are grateful to the following for permission to reproduce copyright material:

4.1.3. Cover image from *The Thing Lou Couldn't Do* written and illustrated by Ashley Spires, cover illustration © 2017 Ashley Spires. Reproduced by permission of Kids Can Press Ltd., Toronto. **5.4.3**, An extract about bullying, NSPCC, https://www.nspcc.org.uk/what-is-child-abuse/types-of-abuse/bullying-and-cyberbullying/. Reproduced with permission; **5.6.3**, "Game age ratings explained", PEGI, copyright © PEGI S.A. Reproduced with permission; and **5.7.2**, Quotes by Sir James Dyson, https://www.dyson.com/james-dyson, copyright © Sir James Dyson, 2011-2023. Reproduced with kind permission.

The Publishers wish to thank the following for permission to reproduce images and copyright material. Every effort has been made to trace copyright holders and to obtain their permission for the use of copyright materials. The publishers will gladly receive any information enabling them to rectify any error or omission at the first opportunity.

4.1.1 SB p. 1 (tl) Vector bucket/ Shutterstock, (tr) StudioBrandShop/ Shutterstock, 4.1.1 (bl) ober-art / Shutterstock, (br) Vector bucket/ Shutterstock, 4.1.1 PPT Slide 1 MillaF/Shutterstock, Slide 3 & SB p. 2 jsabirova/Shutterstock, Slide 4 violetkaipa/Shutterstock, Slide 5 Yury Zap/ Shutterstock, WS 4.1.1a jsabirova/Shutterstock, **4.1.2** PPT Slide 1 Ground Picture/ Shutterstock, Slide 2 (l) PeopleImages.com – Yuri A/ Shutterstock, (tr) Roman Samborskyi/ Shutterstock, (br) anut21ng Stock/ Shutterstock, Slide 3 Gelpi/Shutterstock, Slide 4 YASH GARG FOTOGRAFIE/ Shutterstock, WS 4.1.2b YASH GARG FOTOGRAFIE/ Shutterstock, 4.1.3 PPT Slide 1 & SB p. 8 MinskDesign/ Shutterstock, Slide 2 Cover image from The Thing Lou Couldn't Do written and illustrated by Ashley Spires, cover illustration © 2017 Ashley Spires. Reproduced by permission of Kids Can Press Ltd., Toronto. **4.2.1** PPT Slide 5 Oleg Nesterov/ Shutterstock, Slides 1-5 Reprinted by permission of HarperCollins Publishers Ltd © 2023, Lisa Rajan, **4.2.2** Ealita.ID/ Shutterstock, SB p14 Ealita.ID/ Shutterstock, SB p. 15 Nicoleta Ionescu/ Shutterstock, **4.2.3** WS Nicoleta Ionescu/Shutterstock, PPT Slide 1 Iconic Bestiary/ Shutterstock, Slide 2 (tl) Moosavefoto/ Shutterstock, (t) Monkey Business Images/ Shutterstock, (tr) Africa Studio/ Shutterstock, (bl) Shyamalamuralinath/ Shutterstock, (br) Jacob Lund/ Shutterstock, Slide 3 (tl) Patrick Foto/Shutterstock, (tr) Elena Yakusheva/Shutterstock, (bl) Govind Jangvir/Shutterstock, (br) Daria Medvedeva/Shutterstock, **4.3.1** WS 4.3.1a Jr images/ Shutterstock, SB p. 17 RomanR/ Shutterstock, PPT Slide 1 Tatjana Baibakova/ Shutterstock, Slide 3 Kaspars Grinvalds/ Shutterstock, Slide 7 & SB pp20–21 NIPAPORN PANYACHAROEN/ Shutterstock, Slide 7 & SB pp20–21 MarcoFood/ Shutterstock, Slide 7 & SB pp20–21 Tim UR/ Shutterstock, Slide 7 & SB pp20–21 Ermak Oksana/ Shutterstock, Slide 7 & SB pp20–21 Dionisvera/ Shutterstock, Slide 7 & SB pp20–21 baibaz/ Shutterstock, Slide 7 & SB pp20–21 Craevschii Family/ Shutterstock, Slide 7 & SB pp20–21 New Africa/ Shutterstock, **4.3.2** PPT Slide 1 (r) Daxiao Productions/ Shutterstock, (l) RomanR/ Shutterstock, Slide 2 & SB p. 23 Benjamin Ordaz/ Shutterstock, Slides 3 & 6 inspiring.team/ Shutterstock, SB 4.3.2 inspiring.team/ Shutterstock, **4.3.3** PPT Slide 1 (b) Riccardo Mayer/ Shutterstock, (tl) PeopleImages.com – Yuri A/ Shutterstock, (tr) aslysun/ Shutterstock, Slide 3 Ory Gonian/ Shutterstock, Slide 4 riopatuca/ Shutterstock, Slide 6 yusufdemirci/ Shutterstock, **4.4.1** SB p. 25 (t) Monkey Business Images/Shutterstock, p. 25 (r) Rohit Seth/Shutterstock, p. 25 (b) Monkey Business Images/Shutterstock, p. 26 Athanasia Nomikou/ Shutterstock, **4.4.2** SB p. 28 Athanasia Nomikou/ Shutterstock, WS 4.4.2 Athanasia Nomikou/ Shutterstock, PPT Slide 1 (tl) Sophon Nawit/ Shutterstock, (tr) Rawpixel.com/ Shutterstock, (bl) Denis Kuvaev/ Shutterstock, (br) Ground Picture/ Shutterstock, Slide 2 wavebreakmedia/ Shutterstock, Slide 3 (tl) Prostock-studio/ Shutterstock, (t) Ground Picture/ Shutterstock, (tr) mguttman/ Shutterstock, (bl) Darrin Henry/ Shutterstock, (b) Monkey Business Images/ Shutterstock, (bl) Reshetnikov_art/ Shutterstock, Slide 4 Monkey Business Images/ Shutterstock, **4.4.3** PPT Slides 1 & 2 Rawpixel.com/ Shutterstock, slides 3 & 4 Lemberg Vector studio/ Shutterstock, Slide 5 Dmitry Demidovich / Shutterstock, Slide 6 theshots.co/ Shutterstock, SB p. 32 Svetliy/ Shutterstock, **4.5.1** SB p. 33 (tl) dzejdi/ Shutterstock, (tr) IZZ HAZEL/ Shutterstock, (bl) nikolae/ Shutterstock, (br) TotemArt/ Shutterstock, PPT Slide 4 Ken Cook/ Shutterstock, **4.5.2** PPT Slide 3 ESB Professional/ Shutterstock, Slide 4 & SB p. 36 OlyaOK/ Shutterstock, pp. 37 & 40 Eightshot_Studio / Shutterstock, SB Eightshot_Studio / Shutterstock, **4.5.3** PPT Slide 1 (br) Africa Studio/Adobe Stock, (tr) ilikestudio/ Shutterstock, (bl) vesna cvorovic / Shutterstock, (tl) UfaBizPhoto/ Shutterstock, Slide 2 Littlekidmoment/ Shutterstock, Slide 3 Elena_Dig / Shutterstock, Slide 4 & SB p. 39 Luis Molinero/ Shutterstock, Slide 5 Thinglass / Shutterstock, Slide 6 New Africa / Shutterstock, **4.6.1** SB p41 (tl) cunaplus/ Shutterstock, (tr) Dinesh Hukmani/ Shutterstock, (bl) Fedor Selivanov/ Shutterstock, (br) Motortion Films/ Shutterstock, PPT Slide 1 Kirk Fisher/ Shutterstock, Slides 2 & 5 Gina Kelly / Alamy Stock Photo, **4.6.2** PPT Slide 1 (tl) nik_nadal/ Shutterstock, (tr) ADM Photo / Shutterstock, (bl) fotokaleinar / Shutterstock, (br) vchal / Shutterstock, Slide 2 mindscanner/ Shutterstock, **4.6.3** SB p. 46 hurricanehank/ Shutterstock, WS 4.6.3 hurricanehank/ Shutterstock, PPT Slide 1 Prostock-studio/ Shutterstock, Slide 2 Prostock-studio / Shutterstock, Slide 4 Monkey Business Images / Shutterstock, **4.7.1** SB p. 49 & PPT 4.7.2 Slide 1 (tr) Roman Samborskyi/ Shutterstock, 4.7.1 SB pp. 49 & 54, ChristianChan / Shutterstock, SB p. 49& 4.7.1 PPT Slide 1 imtmphoto / Shutterstock, 4.7.1 PPT Slide 2 Erik Clegg / Shutterstock, 4.7.1 PPT Slide 3 WESTOCK PRODUCTIONS / Shutterstock, 4.7.1 PPT Slide 4 designkida / Shutterstock, 4.7.1 PPT Slide 5 Nach-Noth / Shutterstock, **4.7.2** PPT Slide 1 (l) ChristianChan / Shutterstock, (br) Dina Belenko/ Shutterstock, Slide 2 & SB p. 53 Zainudin_Kho / Shutterstock, WS 4.7.2 Zainudin_Kho / Shutterstock, **4.7.3** PPT Slide 1 Prostock-studio/ Shutterstock,